WHAT ABOUT ME?

STUDY GUIDE

GET OUT OF YOUR OWN WAY AND DISCOVER THE POWER OF AN UNSELFISH LIFE

T0384076

JOYCE MEYER

FaithWords

NEW YORK · NASHVILLE

FaithWords
Hachette Book Group
1290 Avenue of the Americas, New York, NY 10104
faithwords.com
twitter.com/faithwords

First Edition: September 2024

FaithWords is a division of Hachette Book Group, Inc. The FaithWords name and logo are
registered trademarks of Hachette Book Group, Inc.

The publisher is not responsible for websites (or their content) that are not owned by the publisher.

The Hachette Speakers Bureau provides a wide range of authors for speaking events. To find out
more, go to hachettespeakersbureau.com or email HachetteSpeakers@hbgusa.com.

FaithWords books may be purchased in bulk for business, educational, or promotional use. For
information, please contact your local bookseller or the Hachette Book Group Special Markets
Department at special.markets@hbgusa.com.

ISBN: 978-1-5460-4699-8

Printed in the United States of America

LSC-C

Printing 2, 2024

CONTENTS

Introduction   v

PART 1: LEARNING TO LOVE   1

Chapter 1.   I Was Always on My Mind   3

Chapter 2.   Unexpected Joy   8

PART 2: GETTING OUT OF YOUR OWN WAY   15

Chapter 3.   What Do You Want?   17

Chapter 4.   What Do You Think?   22

Chapter 5.   How Do You Feel?   27

PART 3: BECOMING AN OBEDIENT FOLLOWER OF JESUS   33

Chapter 6.   Walking in the Spirit, Part 1   35

Chapter 7.   Walking in the Spirit, Part 2   39

Chapter 8.   The Mind of the Spirit   45

Chapter 9.   The Natural and the Spiritual   50

Chapter 10. Dying to Self   54

Chapter 11. Living to God   59

Chapter 12. Belonging to Christ   66

PART 4: THE UNEXPECTED PATH TO JOY   73

Chapter 13. Declare War on Selfishness   75

Chapter 14. Be Determined and Relentless   82

Chapter 15. Discover the Power of Caring for Others   89

Chapter 16. Fight Greed with Generosity   95

PART 5: "IT'S REALLY NOT ABOUT ME"   101

Chapter 17. For the Love of God   103

Chapter 18. What About Me?   111

Chapter 19. Resurrection Power   116

Chapter 20. This Hurts!   122

Chapter 21. The Living Dead   127

Chapter 22. Complete Surrender   133

Conclusion   139

INTRODUCTION

Years ago, I had a personal relationship with God but seemed to be almost stagnant in my spiritual growth. Even though I had been a believer for a long time, I was still a baby Christian and was selfish, self-centered, and filled with self-pity. I basically lived my life according to three questions: What do I want? What do I think? And how do I feel?

One morning, the Holy Spirit began to help me understand my situation. I envisioned the devil putting this question in my head and repeating it over and over: "What about me?" "What about me?" "What about me?" I came to realize that I must have reminded God of a little robot the devil wound up every morning with selfish thoughts, and all He heard out of me all day long was, "What about me?" "What about me?" "What about me? *Beep. Beep.* What about me?" Through this experience, God showed me in a mere moment just how selfish I was.

Acknowledging that I was a very selfish person was extremely difficult and painful for me, and I think it's hard for everyone. But admitting my self-centeredness and allowing God to deal with it was life-changing for me. If you will acknowledge any selfishness that may be in you and ask God to help you with it, I believe the result will be life-changing for you too. Learning to live an unselfish life may not seem to be a path to happiness and blessing, but I know from firsthand experience that it is.

Living selfishly is like living in solitary confinement. We separate ourselves from others because we are our primary focus and top priority. Then we find ourselves lonely and unhappy in life. We want to be happy, but our selfishness keeps that desire from being fulfilled.

We are born as selfish human beings, but when we are born again, the Holy

Spirit fills our hearts with love and care for others and shows us how to bless them instead of thinking so much about ourselves. The first step on the journey of unselfish living is to *desire* to live free from self-centeredness. We need to *want* to focus on others, to be generous, and to trust God with everything about our lives instead of trying to take care of ourselves and make our own decisions because we think we know what's best. Once we have the desire to leave selfishness behind, we need to *learn* how to be unselfish—because it doesn't come naturally.

This study guide is designed to help you develop the skills and attitudes you need to find your way into the joys of unselfish, others-focused living. The questions will invite you to interact with and process the principles and insights in *What About Me?* so you can apply its teachings to your life.

Let me encourage you to be as honest and vulnerable as possible as you answer the questions in this book. Even if you have to admit some things about yourself that are painful, do it—because that's the way change begins. I know that the journey toward unselfish living isn't always easy. But I also know that the Holy Spirit is eager to help you.

I wrote in the introduction to *What About Me?* that "This book is about learning to love and the joy it brings." And this study guide is a great practical tool that will help you as you learn to love and discover the joys that are waiting for you along the way.

Love,

Joyce

PART 1

Learning to Love

I Was Always on My Mind

Treat others the same way you want them to treat you.

Luke 6:31 AMP

Can you relate to this chapter's title, "I Was Always on My Mind"? In what areas of your life do you feel you think about yourself too much?

_____

_____

Part of learning to love others and live unselfishly is to follow the advice of this chapter's opening scripture, Luke 6:31. In a specific situation in your life, how can you treat someone as you want them to treat you?

_____

_____

Regardless of the way other people view you, do you ever feel a vague sense of unhappiness or emptiness? Has it ever occurred to you that you can find joy in getting your mind off of yourself and onto what you can do to help or bless other people? Explain your answer.

_____

_____

When you read this list, what stands out to you? Circle the one(s) you struggle with. If your struggle is not listed, please write it in the blank below.

- "If I had a better boss, I would be happy."
- "If my kids would just behave, I would be happy."

- "If I could move out of this noisy apartment and buy a house, I would be happy."
- "If my husband would help around the house, I would be happy."
- "If I didn't have so much stress at work, I would be happy."
- "If I could lose weight, I would be happy."
- "If my parents had treated me better when I was growing up, I would be happy."
- "If I could find a way to pursue my dream, I would be happy."
- "If I could finish school, I would be happy."
- "If I could get out of debt, I would be happy."
- Other: _____

Why do you think people typically look to circumstances to identify what needs to change in their lives to make them happy?

_____

_____

What do people around you do that causes you to become angry or feel sorry for yourself?

_____

_____

_____

What does this sentence mean to you, and how can you apply it in your life: "Real love sacrifices for the one it loves"?

_____

_____

_____

In Luke 10:38–42, we read the story of Mary and Martha. Why does Jesus say that Mary made a better choice than Martha? How can you be more like Mary and less like Martha?

_____

_____

_____

Based on the story of Mary and Martha, what is one key to living in peace and enjoying God's presence?

_____

_____

Does any of the behavior described in this section seem like yours? In what ways have you treated people the way I treated them? This may not be easy to admit, but keep in mind that being honest with yourself as you go through this study guide can help you make changes that will lead to great blessings in your life.

_____

_____

The Importance of Living Unselfishly

According to the first sentence of this section, why is living unselfishly important? What does Jesus want for us, according to John 15:11?

_____

_____

Based on John 15:12–13, what is the path to joy?

_____

_____

Fill in the blanks from Philippians 4:5: "Let _____ men know and _____ and recognize your _____ (your considerateness, your forbearing spirit). The Lord is _____ [He is coming soon]."

Is there someone in your life who is difficult to love? Why is it important for you to love them?

_____

_____

According to the first sentence of paragraph 5, what is the result of living for ourselves?

_____

_____

As you take time to think seriously about how selfish you may be, what is God revealing to you about yourself? Remember, don't feel condemned. Be happy when you see something you can work with the Holy Spirit to change in your life, because He always leads you into joy and peace.

_____

_____

How does Matthew 6:33 encourage you on the journey of unselfish living?

_____

_____

"But Really, What About Me?"

What are two important lessons to learn from this section about what living an unselfish life does *not* mean?

_____

_____

What does Psalm 37:4 teach us?

_____

_____

Do you ever allow people to take advantage of you? Why is it important not to let them do this?

_____

_____

What is an important lesson to learn from Philippians 2:4?

_____

_____

How can you take care of yourself and be good to yourself while also learning to live more unselfishly?

_____

_____

In Mark 8:34, what does Jesus say is the key to following Him?

_____

_____

According to Matthew 22:36–40, what is the most important thing we can do?

_____

_____

CHAPTER 2

Unexpected Joy

It is more blessed [and brings greater joy] to give than to receive.

Acts 20:35 AMP

If someone were to ask you, "What would make you happy?" what would your immediate response be?

_____

_____

Why are we more blessed when we give than when we receive what we want?

_____

_____

How does the world we live in reinforce the idea that getting what we want makes us happy?

_____

_____

Fill in the blanks in this sentence from paragraph 3 of this section: "I have heard that some celebrities and other high-profile people have admitted that once they attained or accrued the things _____ wanted, their lives still felt _____. That's because getting what _____ _____ doesn't ultimately leave us _____ in our souls or _____ in our hearts. It only leaves us _____ _____."

What are the five key reasons people become self-focused and greedy instead of unselfish and generous? Why are these called "joy-blockers"?

_____

_____

Are you suffering from some kind of emotional pain? How do you seek relief from this situation? How does this issue cause you to want to focus on yourself rather than on others?

_____

_____

Have you endured some type of deep disappointment? How have you tried to compensate for not getting what you wanted?

_____

_____

Do you feel there is something lacking in your life today? Or did you grow up in an environment of lack? In what ways have you tried to get what you needed and did not have? How much energy do you spend trying to make sure you or your loved ones will not go without what you need?

_____

_____

Do you struggle with fear (including worry, anxiety, and dread)? Why is it difficult to think of other people when you are afraid?

_____

_____

What issues from your childhood could lead to your being selfish as an adult?

_____

_____

Fill in the blanks in these sentences from the second-to-last paragraph of this section: "God will _____ us from all our emotional _____ and _____, and He will make up for anything we have _____ and always

_____ what we need. He will _____ us from _____, and He will _____ and straighten out the _____ _____ that affect us as adults. And if we let Him, He will teach us how to get our minds off of _____ and experience the _____ that comes from thinking of others."

Selfishness Started in the Garden

How did selfishness start with Adam and Eve in the Garden of Eden?

_____

_____

Fill in the blanks in this sentence from the first paragraph of this section: "Even though they could freely eat of all the other trees in the garden, they sinned by _____ to please _____ instead of _____."

How did sin enter the world?

_____

_____

Why are people born with a sin nature?

_____

_____

What does it mean to have a sin nature?

_____

_____

How do we still sin today, just as Adam and Eve sinned centuries ago?

_____

_____

_____

What advice does Proverbs 3:5–6 (NKJV) offer us?

_____

_____

According to James 4:1–2, what leads to strife?

_____

_____

Instead of struggling to get the things we want, what should we do?

_____

_____

_____

Fill in the blanks in this sentence from the last paragraph of this section: "Saying _____ to yourself and _____ to God is not always easy, but it is _____ than living selfishly and caring only for _____."

Whose responsibility is our happiness?

_____

_____

_____

Sow Happiness

If we want to be happy, what do we need to do?

_____

_____

According to God's Word, what is the law of sowing and reaping?

_____

_____

_____

Based on the Parable of the Sower, what does the seed represent? What does the soil represent?

_____

_____

_____

When we hear God's Word, what happens if our hearts are hard?

_____

_____

_____

When we hear God's Word, what happens if we worry and are deceived by riches?

_____

_____

_____

Why does our enemy, Satan, not want us to learn and act on God's Word?

_____

_____

_____

Based on the last paragraph of this section, how can you plant seeds of happiness and reap a harvest of joy?

_____

_____

_____

Commit Your Way

Are you the type of person who wants your own way? How do you know this?

_____

_____

_____

How do you typically respond when you don't get your own way?

_____

_____

In your own words, summarize what Psalm 37:5 means.

_____

_____

Think about a specific situation that you are dealing with in your life right now. How can you commit your way to the Lord in such circumstances?

_____

_____

PART 2

Getting Out of Your Own Way

What Do You Want?

I delight to do Your will, O my God; yes, Your law is within my heart.

Psalm 40:8

According to the first paragraph of chapter 3, what do we need to do if we want to be happy?

_____

_____

What are the three key questions of selfishness?

1. _____
2. _____
3. _____

As long as we live according to what we want, what we think, and what we feel, what two things happen?

_____

_____

Dealing with Desires

Do you have a hard time dealing with desires—"what I want"? How has the experience of not getting what you want caused you to be excessive at times in terms of trying to get what you would like to have?

_____

_____

Why is it true that we cannot simply "move away" from problems in our soul?

_____

_____

Can you understand why being forced to do things against your will or having a controlling person in your life as a child would cause you to insist on getting what you want as an adult? How does this apply to you personally?

_____

_____

Have you realized that we are confronted with authority everywhere we go? Who or what is in authority in your life?

_____

_____

As Christians, what is our ultimate authority?

_____

_____

Why is it important to remember that every action has a reaction?

_____

_____

Fill in the blanks in this sentence from the second-to-last paragraph of this section: "God wants us to use _____ free _____ to _____ His will."

Where do we discover God's will?

_____

_____

First Thessalonians 5:18 clearly states one thing we can do to obey God's will. What is it?

_____

_____

Does God's will include complaining? Why not?

_____

_____

Fill in the blanks in this sentence from the last paragraph of this section: "If we _____ by doing what we know to be God's will for _____, such as being thankful in all circumstances, He will _____ His _____ will concerning _____ situations."

What does Colossians 3:23–24 (NIV) teach us about the attitude we should have as we go about doing what we need to do, even when those tasks are not particularly spiritual?

_____

_____

The Big Boss

The soul is composed of the mind, the will, and the emotions. Which one is "the big boss"? Why?

_____

_____

Why does God sometimes let us have what we want, even if it isn't best for us?

_____

_____

Have you ever thought you really wanted something and discovered after you got it that it wasn't best for you? What happened? What did you learn from this experience?

_____

_____

Give this question some serious thought: Do you really want God's will for your life? If not, pray and ask Him to help you desire His will over your own will.

_____

_____

Have you had to sacrifice in some way because you chose to do God's will? How did God prove Himself faithful to you in that situation? What lessons did you learn as you followed God's leading in your life?

_____

_____

Fill in the blanks in this sentence from paragraph 8 of this section: "Doing God's will is not always _____, but eventually we will see that it is always the _____ for us."

How have you found this statement to be true: "God doesn't waste anything in our lives, not even our pain if we will give it to Him"?

_____

_____

What does it mean that pain digs a deeper place in our soul for God to fill?

_____

_____

Jesus, Our Example

In your own words, based on Matthew 26:36–44 (NIV), how would you describe Jesus' suffering on the cross? As you think about this, remember that He did it for you.

_____

_____

Have you ever gone through something so difficult that you said "I feel like this is going to kill me"? What was the situation? How is God bringing you life in the midst of it?

_____

_____

As the flesh dies to self, what happens to us in the Spirit, according to 1 Peter 3:18?

_____

_____

Can we choose to do the will of God, even if we don't want to? How does Jesus' example on the cross empower us to do this?

_____

_____

What happens to our flesh as we feed on God's Word?

_____

_____

How do the following scriptures strengthen you in your war against the flesh?

- Ephesians 3:16 NIV
- 1 Peter 4:19 NIV
- 1 Peter 3:17 NIV
- Hebrews 10:36 NIV

CHAPTER 4

What Do You Think?

For God has not given us a spirit of fear, but of power and of love and of a sound mind.

2 Timothy 1:7 NKJV

What happens when the mind becomes renewed and changed to agree with God?

_____

_____

_____

What is the result of thinking positively? What is the result of thinking negatively?

_____

_____

_____

You don't have to think whatever comes to your mind. Why is thinking any thought that comes to mind not a good way to live?

_____

_____

_____

What does it mean to have the mind of Christ (1 Corinthians 2:16)?

_____

_____

_____

"Let Me Tell You What I Think..."

How many times would you estimate that you offer your opinion to other people in a typical day?

_____ 1–5 times

_____ 5–10 times

_____ 10–15 times

_____ Too many to count!

When was the last time you noticed yourself giving an opinion about something or someone you know little about and later realized you didn't have all the facts? How can that situation teach you to not state your opinions so freely in the future?

_____

_____

Why are thoughts and words two of the most important topics to study in God's Word?

_____

_____

What kind of thinking leads to misery?

_____

_____

How Many Lies Do You Believe?

Why is it dangerous to believe lies even when we don't know they are lies?

_____

_____

What are some of the lies you think the devil has influenced you to believe?

_____

_____

Why is it important to study God's Word?

_____

_____

How have you seen this quote by Mahatma Gandhi to be true: "A man is but the product of his thoughts, what he thinks he becomes"?

_____

_____

In what ways have you noticed that your thoughts affect every area of your life?

_____

_____

Think on These Things

Read Philippians 4:8. Next to the word(s) from the text, write down how you can incorporate each one into your thoughts:

True: _____

Worthy of reverence: _____

Honorable and seemly (decent): _____

Just: _____

Pure: _____

Lovely and lovable: _____

Kind and winsome (pleasant) and gracious: _____

Virtue and excellence: _____

Worthy of praise: _____

Number the items in the list of twelve ways of thinking that will be beneficial to you according to how much you need to incorporate them into your mindset, with 1 being the most important.

_____ Think every difficulty will end well.

_____ Don't worry.

_____ Think of people's strengths, not their flaws.

_____ Stop rehearsing what's wrong with you.

_____ Don't focus on past mistakes or painful things but look to the good future God has for you.

_____ Don't allow yourself to think self-pitying thoughts.

_____ Think about what you can do to help other people and make them happy.

_____ Keep your mind on what you are doing and learn to be mentally present.

_____ Let your mind be filled with thanksgiving.

_____ Don't compare yourself with others.

_____ Have a humble mind. Don't think too highly of yourself.

_____ Don't dread.

Look at number 1 on your list. Identify specific areas in your life in which you struggle to do it, then pray for God's help in changing your thinking. Focus on this first, then work through the rest of the list in order.

Why? Why? Why?

How much of each day do you spend thinking about why things happen the way they do? How would things change if you were to trust God completely, without any doubts?

_____

_____

In Proverbs 3:5, what does "do not rely on your own insight or understanding" mean to you?

_____

_____

What is a sure sign you have gone too far in reasoning?

_____

Fill in the blanks in these sentences from the last paragraph of this section: "God desires that we _____ Him completely, and we would not need to do that if we _____ all the _____. Digging too _____ into why something happened can open the door to _____."

Exalt God's Word over Your Own Thinking

In your own words, what does it mean to "die to our own thinking"? In what situations do you need to do this?

_____

_____

Job repents for questioning God in Job 42:2–6. What can you learn from his example?

_____

_____

CHAPTER 5

How Do You Feel?

Whoever is slow to anger is better than the mighty, and he who rules his spirit than he who takes a city.

Proverbs 16:32 ESV

Reread Proverbs 16:32 (ESV). What does this Bible verse mean, and why do you believe it is true?

_____

_____

According to the first paragraph of this chapter, why is the question "How do I feel?" so important?

_____

_____

There are good emotions and bad emotions. What should we do with the good ones? How should we handle the bad ones?

_____

_____

Why should we not allow ourselves to be led by how we feel?

_____

_____

Have you ever been in a situation you felt was terrible, but it actually turned out to be good? Describe what happened.

_____

_____

Has anyone made any of the following statements (or similar ones) to you recently? Circle any that apply. Have you made statements such as these about yourself recently? Put a checkmark by those that apply.

_____ "I feel like no one loves me."

_____ "I feel guilty."

_____ "I feel like I don't fit in."

_____ "I feel insecure."

_____ "I feel like I'm not making any progress in overcoming my problems."

_____ "I feel discouraged."

_____ "I feel depressed."

_____ "I feel like giving up."

What is "level emotion," and why is it important?

_____

_____

What are two ways to purposefully increase feel-good emotions?

_____

_____

Why do we all need balance in our lives?

_____

_____

How would you describe your personality type? How does this affect your emotions?

_____

_____

Why is expressing your emotions appropriately when you are hurt or need to grieve important?

_____

_____

How have you been learning to deal with your emotions? Have you ever made a decision based on emotion rather than wisdom? What lesson(s) did you learn from this experience?

_____

_____

Feelings Don't Always Tell Us the Truth

What can happen when we base our decisions on emotions?

_____

_____

Describe a time when you allowed your feelings to cause you to break your word after you'd told someone you would do something.

_____

_____

Why is it important for us not to base our decisions on emotions and to make right decisions no matter how we feel?

_____

_____

Fill in the blanks from Psalm 15:4 (NIV). It is good to be a person who "_____ an oath even when it hurts, and does not _____ their _____."

Have you made any commitments—even seemingly minor ones—that you have not fulfilled? What can you do about that? Can you fulfill the commitment now or at least apologize for not keeping your word?

_____

_____

_____

Dominate Your Emotions

What happens if we don't dominate our emotions?

_____

_____

Fill in the blanks in this sentence from the first paragraph of this section: "Emotions are a _____ force, and _____ ones are often the culprits behind most of our _____."

Why are teenagers especially vulnerable to emotions?

_____

_____

Complete this sentence from paragraph 3 of this section: "You may not be able to control how you feel, but you can control _____ _____ _____."

What is the difference between denying emotions and refusing to let them control us?

_____

_____

Catering to the Flesh

What does it mean to cater to the flesh?

_____

_____

Fill in the blanks from Romans 8:13–14: "For if you live according to [the dictates of] the _____, you will surely

die. But if through the _____ of the [Holy]
_____ you are [habitually] putting to death (making
extinct, deadening) the [evil] deeds prompted by the body, you shall
[really and genuinely] _____ forever. For all who
are _____ by the Spirit of God are sons of God."

What happens to harmful emotions if we do not keep feeding them?

_____

_____

What is the result of doing what is right when we feel like doing what is
wrong?

_____

_____

According to the amplification of 1 Corinthians 3:3, why were the Corinthi-
ans "unspiritual"?

_____

_____

Why is living by the emotion of anger an unpleasant and dangerous way to
live?

_____

_____

_____

Based on 2 Corinthians 2:10–11, why should we forgive people we are angry
toward and people who have hurt us?

_____

_____

_____

Why is it to our benefit to forgive?

_____

_____

_____

When I Want to Do Good, Evil Always Comes

Describe a time when you wanted to do what's right but ended up doing what's wrong instead.

_____

_____

What did Paul mean by the "sin [principle]" in Romans 7:20?

_____

_____

In your own words, what does Romans 8:1 mean to you personally?

_____

_____

When we fail to do what is right, what are the two ways we can handle it? What happens if we continue walking in the flesh? What happens if we choose to walk in the Spirit?

_____

_____

According to the third-to-last paragraph of this chapter, what is sanctification?

_____

_____

Why do we not have to live in guilt and condemnation?

_____

_____

When we fail, why should we follow the example of a toddler who is learning to walk?

_____

_____

PART 3

Becoming an Obedient Follower of Jesus

CHAPTER 6
Walking in the Spirit, Part 1

I say then: Walk in the Spirit, and you will not fulfill the lust of the flesh.

Galatians 5:16 NKJV

Walking in the Spirit isn't something we can do automatically simply because we are believers. It is something we must seek with ardent zeal, pray about, learn, and practice. What are you doing to incorporate this into your daily life?

_____

_____

One way to walk in the Spirit is to obey the Holy Spirit's promptings. Can you remember a time when you did this? What happened?

_____

_____

According to Galatians 5:16, what will happen if you focus on walking in the Spirit?

_____

_____

True or false: The best way to live a godly life is to focus on defeating your temptations. Explain your answer.

_____

_____

Fill in the blanks in this sentence from paragraph 2 of this section: "If we are doing the _____ thing, there is no _____ in our life for the _____ thing."

What impressed you the most about Susan's story? In your life, when have you found it helpful to focus more on others than yourself?

_____

_____

The Struggle to Resist the Flesh

Explain what this Derek Prince quote means to you: "Endeavoring to live the Christian life by your own efforts is the greatest single hindrance to walking in the Spirit."

_____

_____

Based on Zechariah 4:6 (NKJV), why can't you resist the flesh by your own efforts?

_____

_____

What are some of the attitudes or behaviors you are trying to overcome in your own strength? Once you identify them, ask God to help you overcome them.

_____

_____

It's easy to focus on how far you have to go, rather than how far you've come. What are some areas in which God has helped you gain victory?

_____

_____

Have you ever tried to change someone else's behavior? How did that work out?

_____

_____

If you have been waiting for a while for God to change you but haven't seen any results, what could be some reasons for the delay? Read 1 Peter 5:5 and James 4:2 for clues.

_____

_____

In your own words, what does this statement mean: "Only God can change people, because real change happens from the inside out, not from the outside in"? How have you experienced this personally?

_____

_____

_____

What does "from one degree of glory to another" mean in 2 Corinthians 3:18?

_____

_____

_____

What are some specific ways you have asked God to change you? When you pray, tell Him you know He is working on each one and that you are trusting Him to do what needs to be done.

_____

_____

_____

Think of someone who has hurt you. What could you do to bless them to break the power of any negative feelings you have toward them? Choose one or more of the following or add your own and decide to take action.

- Pray for them—an interesting exercise is to pray for them in the first person as if praying for yourself and see what comes to mind.
- Buy them a gift.
- Do something nice for them.
- Give them a compliment.
- Other:_____

Cooperating with the Holy Spirit

What do you need to do to cooperate with the Holy Spirit in an area in which you need to change? Why doesn't God just go ahead and make the change in you?

_____

_____

Read the A. B. Simpson quote in paragraph 2 of this section. What does it teach you about how God works along with human free will?

_____

_____

Fill in the blanks in this sentence from the second-to-last paragraph of this chapter: "Even though we turn a situation over to _____, we still have a _____ to _____ with the Holy Spirit as He _____ and _____ us."

What are some ways you can cooperate with the Holy Spirit more in your life over the next weeks and months?

_____

_____

CHAPTER 7

Walking in the Spirit, Part 2

If we live in the Spirit, let us also walk in the Spirit.

Galatians 5:25 NKJV

Fill in the blanks from the first sentence of this chapter: "Walking in the
_____ does not come with a list of _____
to follow; it is something we do based on how He _____
us at any given _____."

What is the best way to know what the Holy Spirit approves of?

_____

_____

_____

Describe a time when you knew you were walking in the Spirit because of
the peace He gave you.

_____

_____

_____

What does being "changed into the image of Jesus Christ" mean? What
enables us to be changed into the image of Jesus Christ?

_____

_____

_____

Enjoy Yourself While You Change

How can you enjoy where you are on the way to where you're going?

_____

_____

Have you ever thought God can't use you? Explain your answer. Why is that not true?

_____

_____

Based on 2 Corinthians 5:21, how does God view you? Why?

_____

_____

Why is it so important for us to learn who we are in Christ?

_____

_____

Why does God want us to love ourselves in a balanced way?

_____

On a scale of 1–10, with 1 being "very easy" and 10 being "very difficult," how easy is it for you to love yourself in a healthy way? Circle the number you feel best represents how hard or easy it is and explain why.

_1 2 3 4 5 6 7 8 9 10_

Do you focus more on your weaknesses and shortcomings than on your strengths and the things you do well? Why?

_____

_____

List three or four positive things about yourself.

1. _____

2. _____

3. _____

4. _____

What can you do today, this week, this month, and this year to enjoy your life more than you are enjoying it right now?

_____

_____

What does Jesus teach in Matthew 22:39?

_____

_____

The Difference between Spirit and Flesh

List five key differences between the Holy Spirit and the flesh.

1. _____

2. _____

3. _____

4. _____

5. _____

What kinds of decisions do you have to make each day in order to keep walking in the Spirit and resist walking in the flesh?

_____

_____

The Fruit and Gifts of the Holy Spirit

According to Galatians 5:22–23, what are the nine fruits of the Holy Spirit?

1. _____

2. _____

3. _____

4. _____

5. _____

6. _____

7. _____

8. _____

9. _____

Because of personality, temperament, and the ways God has wired each of us, certain fruit of the Holy Spirit may seem easier to develop than others, even though the Holy Spirit is constantly helping us grow in each one. Perhaps you know what I mean. For example, some people are more joyful than others, and some are more patient. Which fruit of the Holy Spirit tends to come naturally to you? Which ones do you have to intentionally develop? What does it mean to bear fruit?

_____

_____

The fruit of the Holy Spirit and the gifts of the Holy Spirit are not the same. List the spiritual gifts mentioned in Romans 12:6–8 and 1 Corinthians 12:4–11 (NKJV) and circle the ones you believe God has given you:

- _____

- practical _____

- _____

- _____ (referred to as "encouragement" in the New International Version)

- _____ (referred to as "giving" in the New International Version)
- _____ (referred to in terms of leadership in the New International Version)
- acts of _____
- word of _____
- word of _____
- _____
- gifts of _____
- working of _____
- _____
- discerning of _____
- different kinds of _____
- _____ of tongues

Do you believe God has given you any spiritual gifts not listed above? If so, what are they?

_____

_____

Stay in Your Lane

Have you ever tried to do something God has not gifted you to do? Did you enjoy it? What was the result?

_____

_____

Fill in the blanks in this sentence from the first paragraph of this section: "When we stay within our _____, we express them with _____ because the Holy Spirit _____ us."

Paul encourages us in 1 Timothy 4:13–16 to give ourselves to our gift. What is one of your gifts, and how could you give yourself to it in practical ways?

_____

_____

If you are not expressing or exercising the gifts God has given you, what's holding you back? Ask God to help you find ways to do what He has gifted you to do.

_____

_____

Lessons from the School of the Holy Spirit

Describe a time when you felt that you were attending the school of the Holy Spirit. What lessons did you learn?

_____

_____

How have you recently noticed the guidance or teaching of the Holy Spirit in the everyday, ordinary aspects of your life?

_____

_____

In what area of your life is God dealing with you right now? Are you tempted to make excuses? Explain your answer.

_____

_____

How has God taught you integrity through the tasks of everyday life?

_____

_____

CHAPTER 8

The Mind of the Spirit

The mind governed by the flesh is death, but the mind governed by the Spirit is life and peace.

Romans 8:6 NIV

Reread Romans 8:6 (NIV). Based on what you've learned in *What About Me?*, why do you believe this verse is true?

_____

_____

Explain this statement: "Bad thoughts produce bad feelings." Describe a time when you found this to be true.

_____

_____

Think about a challenge or a problem in your life. What would Jesus think about this situation?

_____

_____

Set Your Mind

In your own words, what does it mean to "set your minds on things above, not on earthly things" in Colossians 3:2 (NIV)?

_____

_____

In what specific ways or situations could you think about "things above" today?

_____

_____

What will happen to you if you set your mind on the things of the flesh? Fill in the blanks from this statement in the last paragraph of this section for the answer: "Whatever we set our _____ on, we will _____ _____."

A New Attitude in Your Mind

According to Ephesians 4:22–24, what is the key to putting off the old self and putting on the new self?

_____

_____

How does the following statement seem contrary to the way the world tells you to change yourself: "If we want to behave differently, we have to think differently"?

_____

_____

Describe a time when you tried to change yourself by changing your behavior first. How successful were you?

_____

_____

Is there a behavior or attitude that you are asking God to change in you right now? Are you bold enough to ask Him to do what He wants in you and to give you the strength not to resist Him, but to cooperate with Him? Write this out in a prayer and read it often.

_____

_____

What can you learn about walking in love from these scriptures, and how does each one help you as you are breaking free from the power of selfishness?

- Matthew 22:37–40 NIV
- Philippians 2:4 ESV
- 1 John 3:17 ESV
- Hebrews 13:16 ESV
- Luke 6:38 ESV
- Ephesians 4:32 ESV

Learning to Want What God Wants

What was the difference between Peter's reaction to God's will in Matthew 16:22–23 and Jesus' reaction to God's will in Matthew 26:39? How did selfishness contribute to Peter's failure?

_____

_____

_____

Describe a time when you chose to do God's will instead of your own and suffered for it. How did you feel about the sacrifice you made?

_____

_____

_____

Changed by Renewing the Mind

What is the one essential way to completely renew your mind and learn to think as God does? How do you plan to incorporate this into your life each day?

_____

_____

_____

What is the first thing you have to change to be able to change your behavior?

_____

_____

_____

In what ways have you become less selfish since you began your relationship with Christ?

_____

_____

_____

What does it mean to "die to self"? Fill in the blanks in this sentence from the last paragraph of this section: "Dying to _____ means that although you have a _____ that wants to follow its desires, a _____ that wants to think your own thoughts, and _____ that want you to let them lead you, you can say _____ to all these and _____ to live God's way."

We Want to Know

As you have walked in the Spirit, in what areas have you noticed yourself reasoning less and having more of God's peace about not knowing everything?

_____

_____

_____

What can you learn from 1 Corinthians 2:2 and Philippians 3:10 about what you should focus on instead of excessive reasoning?

_____

_____

_____

Describe a time when you have been deceived by a false belief. How did you feel when you found out the truth?

_____

_____

_____

James 1:22 says that even Christians can be deceived. Why is taking personal responsibility instead of offering excuses vital to spiritual maturity?

_____

_____

_____

CHAPTER 9

The Natural and the Spiritual

The natural person does not accept the things of the Spirit of God, for they are folly to him, and he is not able to understand them because they are spiritually discerned. The spiritual person judges all things, but is himself to be judged by no one.

1 Corinthians 2:14–15 ESV

Why is it that the natural (nonspiritual) person doesn't understand the spiritual person?

_____

_____

_____

Describe a time when you have been in a situation where you tried to follow God's leading and someone around you did not understand.

_____

_____

_____

_____

What in God's Word doesn't make sense to your natural mind? Do you believe God's Word anyway? Why or why not?

_____

_____

_____

What is your attitude toward what God instructs you to do? Do you obey, as Peter did? Or, do you allow your thoughts to influence you away from obeying God?

_____

_____

Hearing from God

Do you believe you can hear from God? Why or why not?

_____

_____

Why should we be especially careful about hearing from God regarding something we strongly want to do?

_____

_____

Have you chosen not to follow God's leading and then suffered the consequences? What lesson or lessons did you learn from that experience?

_____

_____

When we face consequences because we don't follow God's leading, we should not view them as God's punishment. How should we view them?

_____

_____

What does Hebrews 12:6 (NKJV) teach us?

_____

_____

Fill in the blanks in this sentence from the last paragraph of this section: "Don't be so _____ of making a _____ that you won't venture out into learning how to _____ from God, and how to be led by _____ instead of by your natural mind."

Discernment

What is discernment?

_____

_____

A discerning person is considered to have what two qualities?

_____

_____

What is the discerning of spirits, which Paul mentions in 1 Corinthians 12:10? When people have this spiritual gift, what do they know?

_____

_____

Why is discernment so important in the world today?

_____

_____

Have you ever been in a situation in which everything looked or seemed right, but you felt in your spirit that something was wrong? Describe what happened.

_____

_____

How would you summarize Colossians 3:15 (AMPC) in your own words? What does it mean to let peace act as an umpire in your life?

_____

_____

How can we develop greater discernment?

_____

_____

What decisions are you committed to praying about in your life?

_____

_____

In addition to praying about major decisions, it is also wise not to rush to make commitments. Fill in the blanks from this sentence in the second-to-last paragraph of this section: "Whether it is one _____ or a few _____, _____ a little while is much better than making an irreversible _____ that will cause _____ or difficulty, perhaps for _____."

Emotions Fluctuate

Why is it a mistake to make a decision based on emotions alone?

_____

_____

Fill in the blanks in this sentence from the first paragraph of this section: "Let emotions _____ and then _____."

Have you reached the point where what you *think* you can do is different than what you can *actually* do? How can you use wisdom to avoid committing to things you shouldn't obligate yourself to do?

_____

_____

When you need to make a decision, what is the best course of action to take?

_____

_____

CHAPTER 10

Dying to Self

Then he said to them all: "Whoever wants to be my disciple must deny themselves and take up their cross daily and follow me."

Luke 9:23 NIV

Reread Luke 9:23. What does this verse mean to you and what can you do to obey it this week?

_____

_____

What is another way of saying "the flesh"?

_____

_____

What are the three questions selfish people ask? Underline the one-letter word all three of these have in common.

1. _____

2. _____

3. _____

How does focusing on what we want, think, and feel combine to make for a very selfish life?

_____

_____

How often do you think or say something like "What about me?" in the course of a day?

_____

Think about the past few weeks of your life. What are some specific situations that have tempted you to ask "What about me?"

_____

_____

The Spirit and the Word Help Us Die to Self

What does it mean to feed the flesh? What are some ways in which you are tempted to do this?

_____

_____

What does it mean to "put the flesh to death"?

_____

_____

You cannot put the flesh to death by willpower alone. What is needed in order to do it?

_____

_____

"Dying to self" is another way of saying growing into spiritual maturity or being transformed into the image of Christ (Romans 8:29). Why is being transformed into the image of Christ important?

_____

_____

True or false: Our flesh tells us what God's will is.
What are two ways we know God's will?

_____

_____

Do you ever find it hard to see yourself as "dead to sin but alive to God in Christ Jesus" (Romans 6:11 NIV)? If so, what gets in the way of your believing this?

_____

_____

Do you see yourself as Christ says you are? Or do you see yourself according to the way you behave? Explain your answer.

_____

_____

Why do you believe this statement is true: "Your behavior will not change until your beliefs about yourself change"?

_____

_____

Fill in the blanks in this sentence from the last paragraph of this section: "We must learn to believe _____ _____ more than we believe what we _____." How can you do this in practical ways?

_____

_____

What are some of the promises in God's Word you still struggle to believe?

_____

_____

Remember the Israelites

What does it mean that when the Israelites came out of Egypt, Egypt was still in them?

_____

_____

Why do you think the Israelites would have wanted to go back into slavery and bondage instead of pressing through the difficulties in order to reach freedom?

_____

_____

Have you ever felt tempted to "return to Egypt" when you've encountered challenges in your Christian life? What were the circumstances, and what did you do?

_____

_____

What lessons can you learn from the Israelites' negative example?

_____

_____

How did God teach the Israelites to trust Him?

_____

_____

In what ways are you learning to live in the freedom that Christ has given you?

_____

_____

If you still feel you are living in some kind of captivity instead of in the full freedom you have in Christ, what can you do to move toward greater freedom?

_____

_____

Study and Understand

Why is deep study important to understanding the idea of being dead to sin?

_____

_____

As a reminder, resources to help you study the Book of Romans are available in print and/or online from the following authors:

- Matthew Henry
- Warren Wiersbe

- D. L. Moody
- Charles Spurgeon
- Martyn Lloyd-Jones

Why do you think the topic of being dead to sin isn't taught often in most churches? Why is it so important?

_____

_____

CHAPTER 11

Living to God

I have been crucified with Christ [in Him I have shared His crucifixion]; it is no longer I who live, but Christ (the Messiah) lives in me; and the life I now live in the body I live by faith in (by adherence to and reliance on and complete trust in) the Son of God, Who loved me and gave Himself up for me.

Galatians 2:20

In your own words, what does Galatians 2:20 mean to you?

_____

_____

Is it encouraging to you to know that it takes time and experience with God to be able to say "It is no longer I who live, but Christ (the Messiah) lives in me" (Galatians 2:20)? Why?

_____

_____

What does it mean that in Christ we are dead to sin?

_____

_____

_____

Instead of praying we won't be tempted to sin, how should we pray?

_____

_____

_____

What is a common temptation for you, and how can you deal with it aggressively?

_____

_____

Stop Thinking about It

Why is it so important to stop thinking about the sins that tempt us?

_____

_____

Please reread Philippians 3:13–14 (NIV): "Brothers and sisters, I do not consider myself yet to have taken hold of it. But one thing I do: Forgetting what is behind and straining toward what is ahead, I press on toward the goal to win the prize for which God has called me heavenward in Christ Jesus." What is behind you that you need to forget?

_____

_____

How have you experienced the emotional pain of dying to self? What was that like?

_____

_____

_____

How have you found these sentences to be true: "No one enjoys not getting their way, but following God's will is always better in the long run. In the process of giving up what we want, we don't realize that God's way will be better than what we currently have. The longer we are on the journey of dying to self, the more we do realize that God's way is better, even if we don't understand it at the time"?

_____

_____

_____

On your journey of dying to self, how can your thoughts be your keys to victory?

_____

_____

When you are tempted to sin, why is it important to think beyond the temporary pleasure it could bring to you and see the consequences that may result?

_____

_____

It can be helpful to speak aloud to yourself when you are being strongly tempted. What could you say to yourself next time you face temptation?

_____

_____

Selfishness Leads to a Lonely Life

Why does selfishness lead to a lonely life?

_____

_____

Fill in the blanks from John 12:24: "I assure you, most solemnly I tell you, Unless a grain of wheat falls into the earth and _____, it remains [just one grain; it never becomes more but lives] by itself _____. But if it _____, it produces many others and yields a rich _____."

Why must we die to self (selfishness)?

_____

_____

In what areas of your life have you died to self? What joys or blessings resulted from it?

_____

_____

According to the last sentence of this section, what is the key to true happiness?

_____

_____

Lonely in a Crowd

Have you ever experienced feeling lonely even when you were in a crowd, surrounded by people? Explain your answer.

_____

_____

What kind of life does someone who is focused on themselves live?

_____

_____

Pride

What is the root of all selfishness?

_____

_____

What do prideful people think?

_____

_____

What does true humility mean?

_____

_____

_____

What does 1 Peter 5:6 teach about people who are humble?

_____

_____

_____

How often do you think about others compared to how often you think about yourself?

_____

_____

In what ways could you think less about yourself and more about others?

_____

_____

Why does selfish pride lead to arrogance?

_____

_____

According to the last paragraph of this section, what are some signs of having a problem with pride?

_____

_____

Jesus Died So We Could Be Free from Selfishness

What does 2 Corinthians 5:15 say about Jesus' death?

_____

_____

Have you ever been selfish in a situation in which someone was trying to extend kindness to you? Describe what happened.

_____

_____

Author Stephen Kendrick says, "Almost every sinful action ever committed can be traced back to a selfish motive. It's a trait we hate in other people but justify in ourselves." How have you justified selfish motives in yourself, while hating this tendency in other people?

_____

_____

_____

Who Is the Greatest?

Why is it encouraging to realize that even Jesus' disciples were selfish at times?

_____

_____

Helping and serving others does not come naturally to a lot of us. How can you intentionally become more thoughtful and helpful toward the people around you?

_____

_____

How have you seen this statement to be true: "Selfishness is a disease that afflicts all of us in one way or another"?

_____

_____

What are some practical ways you could "die to self, and live wholly to Him"?

_____

_____

What Are You Full Of?

The apostle Paul prays in Ephesians 3:19: "[That you may really come] to know [practically, through experience for yourselves] the love of Christ, which far surpasses mere knowledge [without experience]; that you may be filled [through all your being] unto all the fullness of God [may have the richest measure of the divine Presence, and become a body wholly filled and flooded with God Himself]!" What does this verse mean to you personally? What would it look like for your life to become "wholly filled and flooded with God Himself"?

_____

_____

What is one of your areas of weakness when it comes to wanting what you want? Why do you think getting what you want in this area is so important to you?

_____

_____

How much energy do you expend trying to get what you want? What changes could you make in this area?

_____

_____

Stay Out of Strife

Do you trust God with your desires—not only with the things you want but also with the timing and the way in which He responds to your desires? Why or why not? If you struggle in this area, remember Psalm 37:4: "Delight yourself also in the Lord, and He will give you the desires and secret petitions of your heart."

_____

_____

How can strife result from wanting things and trying to get them for ourselves?

_____

_____

What are some ways you are trying to get things for yourself, in your own strength, instead of simply asking God for what you need?

_____

_____

CHAPTER 12

Belonging to Christ

Those who belong to Christ Jesus have crucified the flesh with its passions and desires.

Galatians 5:24 NIV

What does the Bible mean when it refers to "the flesh"? And what does it mean to crucify the flesh (Galatians 5:24)?

_____

_____

_____

The flesh (our sin nature) is expressed in several ways. How have you seen your flesh expressed through the following?

- Your body
- Your mind
- Your will (meaning your desires and choices)
- Your emotions

What can you learn about your life with Christ from each of these scriptures?

- Philippians 2:1 NIV
- John 17:21
- 1 Corinthians 6:19

What do these Bible verses teach you about being holy?

- 1 Peter 1:15
- 2 Corinthians 5:21
- Hebrews 10:10

Philemon 6 (NKJV) says, "That the sharing of your faith may become effective by the acknowledgment of every good thing which is in you in Christ Jesus." What are some of the good things that are in you because you belong to Christ?

_____

_____

What happens as we give the Holy Spirit access to our soul?

_____

_____

Because you are in Christ, having received Him as your Lord and Savior, how does God view you?

_____

_____

Explain this statement: "Jesus can be our Savior without being our Lord." Do you relate to Him as both Savior and Lord?

_____

_____

What choice do we make when Jesus is Lord in our lives?

_____

_____

What is the one thing we can never say when Jesus is our Lord?

_____

_____

What is the only correct answer to any request from God?

_____

_____

In your own words, what does John 15:5 (NIV) mean?

_____

_____

What have you tried to change in your own strength and realized that you cannot do it? How can you surrender these situations or people to God?

_____

_____

Cooperate with the Holy Spirit

Why was the Holy Spirit sent to earth?

_____

_____

Think of a problem you are struggling with right now. Which of the Holy Spirit's ministries could help you in this situation? Check all that apply.

_____ Helping

_____ Teaching truth

_____ Leading and guiding

_____ Convicting and convincing

_____ Helping us pray

_____ Advocating before God

_____ Comforting

Since the Holy Spirit requires your cooperation to change you, what are some ways you can surrender to Him daily?

_____

_____

What is the difference between life before surrendering to the Holy Spirit and life afterward?

_____

According to 1 Peter 4:1–2, why is suffering necessary in the Christian life? What benefit does it bring?

_____

_____

Why must true change be an "inside job"?

_____

_____

Complete this sentence from paragraph 5 in this section: "God hasn't called us to _____ _____ but to _____."

How will people know we have changed?

_____

_____

Character and the Fruit of the Spirit Must Be Developed

Paul told the Corinthian believers they were carnal (worldly), yet they were born again, baptized in the Holy Spirit, and operating in the gifts of the Spirit. How is it possible that they were also carnal?

_____

_____

What four things are necessary for the fruit of the Spirit to be developed in us?

1. _____

2. _____

3. _____

4. _____

Describe a time when you have seen someone highly gifted fail due to poor character. What do you think may have been missing from their spiritual development?

_____

_____

In your own words, what does 1 Corinthians 3:1–3 mean?

_____

_____

Do You Need a Change?

How have you found this statement to be true: "Often, we want our lives to change, but _we_ don't want to change"?

_____

_____

Are _you_ willing to change? Is there any area of your life in which you are resisting change?

_____

_____

What are several ways the Holy Spirit may deal with you?

_____

_____

Identify an area in which the Holy Spirit is working with you right now. What is a specific Bible verse you can study on this topic?

_____

_____

Do you believe that no one has as many problems as you do? Explain your answer. Remember that everyone has issues, and we all need the Holy Spirit's help to deal with them.

_____

_____

When we have problems in our soul, we usually have problems with people too. What type of "soul problems" would create relationship difficulties? When have you ever experienced this?

_____

_____

Fill in the blanks in this sentence from the second-to-last paragraph of this section: "But the good news is that _____ will give you _____ over those _____ if you are willing to do things _____ way instead of _____."

What does Matthew 19:26 say?

_____

_____

How does Romans 8:28 encourage you as you think about the process of change God needs to take you through?

_____

_____

PART 4

The Unexpected Path to Joy

CHAPTER 13

Declare War on Selfishness

For wherever there is jealousy (envy) and contention (rivalry and selfish ambition), there will also be confusion (unrest, disharmony, rebellion) and all sorts of evil and vile practices.

James 3:16

According to James 3:16, what else can you invite into your life if you allow selfishness to remain?

_____

_____

How have you seen envy and selfish ambition in your own life? What has happened as a result?

_____

_____

When you think of selfishness, which people from the Bible come to mind? Why? What were the consequences of their selfishness?

_____

_____

Several people mentioned in the New Testament acted selfishly. How did Jesus treat them?

_____

_____

True or false: God will give up on you if you're selfish. Explain your answer.

_____

What happened to Peter even after he denied knowing Jesus three times?

_____

_____

What happened to the apostle Paul (previously called Saul) after he participated in the stoning of Stephen and after he persecuted Christians (Acts 9:1–18; 22:20)?

_____

_____

What does Hebrews 4:15 (NIV) teach you about Jesus?

_____

_____

How does Hebrews 4:16 encourage you if you have committed many sins, made many mistakes, and suffered many failures thus far in your life?

_____

_____

Fill in the blanks in this sentence from the last paragraph of this section: "Don't ever _____ that God can't _____ you because you have made _____."

The Good Samaritan

What did the Good Samaritan have to sacrifice to help the injured man?

_____

_____

True or false: Jesus only asks us to do things when it is convenient for us. Explain your answer.

_____

_____

Under what circumstances have you been like the religious men who passed by on the other side of the road?

_____

_____

Think of some instances when Jesus allowed people to interrupt Him. What can these situations teach you about being more available?

_____

_____

Do you currently need to agree to being inconvenienced in order to help someone who needs help? What are the circumstances?

_____

_____

What is your reaction when you see someone asking for help or assistance? Check all that apply.

_____ Avoid them by crossing the street

_____ Walk past them but avoid eye contact

_____ Give them something out of guilt

_____ Assess their condition to decide if they are truly needy

_____ Help them with money or buy them a meal

_____ Pray about whether to help

Why is it not being selfish if you do not help everyone you know or everyone you see who has a need?

_____

_____

When have you found this statement to be true: "If the devil can't get me to do nothing, he will try to get me to do too much"?

_____

_____

What three qualities does God want us to use when deciding whether to help someone?

1. _____
2. _____
3. _____

A Time for Everything

What's the difference between the way we respond when people ask us to do something and the way we need to respond when God asks us?

_____

_____

If we obey God when He asks us to do something, what can we expect from Him?

_____

_____

Fill in the blanks in this sentence from paragraph 2 of this section: "If you want to _____ God with all your _____, get ready to be _____ at times."

How do you interpret Proverbs 16:9 (NIV)? When have you seen this in action?

_____

_____

_____

Why is it a good idea to have a plan but also to make our plans secondary to God's plans for us?

_____

_____

_____

Are you bold enough to tell the Lord that you are willing to let Him interrupt you anytime He wants to and that you will lay aside your plan and follow His? Why or why not?

_____

_____

How have you seen God use your obedience to change your life and the lives of the people you love?

_____

_____

When Jesus called His disciples, they were all doing something else, but they left to follow Him. What would you do if God called you into ministry in some way?

_____

_____

Fill in the blanks in this sentence from the third-to-last paragraph of this section: "Don't _____ yourself to _____ for His _____ unless you are willing to be _____."

How did the prophets Hosea and Isaiah display extreme obedience? What were the purposes of what God asked them to do?

_____

_____

Prefer Others above Yourself

What are some ways you have applied Romans 12:10 to your life? Check all that apply.

_____ Letting others go ahead of me at the grocery store
_____ Giving up a parking space
_____ Listening vs. doing all the talking

_____ Giving someone else the remote

_____ Giving credit to anyone who helped me on a project

_____ Letting people merge in ahead of me in traffic

Other: _____

Which do you choose when you have to decide whether to be kind to someone or to be on time? Which would Jesus choose?

_____

_____

How has selfishness thwarted something Jesus asked you to do?

_____

_____

What does this statement mean: "The flesh never runs out of excuses to avoid doing what God wants us to do"?

_____

_____

What does God want instead of our excuses?

_____

_____

These characteristics of people in the last days from 2 Timothy 3:1–5 have their root in selfishness. Circle the ones you have noticed recently.

- lovers of self
- lovers of money
- proud and arrogant
- abusive
- disobedient to parents
- ungrateful
- unholy
- heartless
- unappeasable

- slanderous
- without self-control
- brutal
- not loving good
- treacherous
- reckless
- swollen with conceit
- lovers of pleasure rather than lovers of God
- having the appearance of godliness but denying its power

How can you be a light in the midst of these things in our world today? Check all that apply:

_____ Use my money to spread the gospel and help people who are hurting

_____ Be humble

_____ Obey authority

_____ Show gratitude

_____ Live a holy life

_____ Love others

_____ Forgive

_____ Believe the best of everyone

_____ Exercise self-control

_____ Be kind

_____ Love good

_____ Be gentle

_____ Be careful and prudent

_____ Love God more than anything

_____ Display the power of the gospel

What is your honest assessment of how you represent Jesus in society? Are there ways in which you could do better? If so, what are they?

_____

CHAPTER 14

Be Determined and Relentless

*Let us not grow weary or become discouraged in doing good, for at the
proper time we will reap, if we do not give in.*

Galatians 6:9 AMP

Regarding selfishness and looking out for one's self, how are the values of
God's kingdom different from the world's values?

_____

_____

_____

What is our handbook on how to live if we want to please God, be happy,
enjoy peace, have good relationships, and prosper in all we do?

_____

_____

_____

Fill in the blanks in this sentence from paragraph 2 of this
section: "One of the most important _____ I have
learned in God's Word is that to be _____ is to be
_____."

How has selfishness led to misery in your life?

_____

_____

Fill in the blanks: Matthew 22:37–40 teaches us to love God with all our

_____, _____, _____,

and _____. This passage also teaches us to love our

neighbor as we love _____. Can we do this if we are

filled with selfishness? Why or why not?

_____

_____

Why does defeating selfishness require us to change?

_____

_____

Have you encountered Christians who do not really want to change and grow? On a scale of 1–10, with 1 being "not much" and 10 being "very much," how much do you honestly want to change and grow?

1 2 3 4 5 6 7 8 9 10

What are some ways you could put God's kind of sacrificial love into action with someone you don't like?

_____

_____

Are You Determined?

What does David pray in Psalm 51:10? Are you willing to pray this same prayer for yourself?

_____

_____

When have you demonstrated each of these qualities when trying to accomplish something:

- Endurance
- Perseverance

- Effort
- Determination
- Relentlessness
- Steadfastness

Why is determination vital in order to have a successful life?

_____

_____

True or false: God works through us, but He won't do everything for us. Explain your answer.

_____

_____

In Philippians 3:10–11, why was Paul so willing to share in Christ's sufferings? How have you seen this attitude in a fellow believer? Do you have this attitude in yourself?

_____

_____

Are you wasting time feeling guilty about things for which God has forgiven you? How can you receive His forgiveness so you can be free and move forward?

_____

_____

Success and Victory Demand Determination

How did Daniel show determination in Daniel 1:8? Have you ever had to refuse to do something the world wanted you to do in order to obey God? What were the circumstances?

_____

_____

List all the things the apostle Paul had to endure to remain determined to preach the Word of God (2 Corinthians 11:23–29), in addition to other things:

1. _____

2. _____

3. _____

4. _____

5. _____

6. _____

Fill in the blanks in these sentences from the last paragraph of this section: "To be _____ you must never _____ _____ or _____ _____. Be _____ and _____, and keep up the _____ required to reach the _____ _____."

Ask and Receive

Read Mark 11:24 and fill in the blanks in this sentence from the first paragraph of this section:

"Anything we ask for must be based on _____ _____, but if it is, God promises we will _____ it."

Why do you usually have to wait for what you ask for?

_____

_____

What are you waiting for right now? Are you waiting with patience and trusting God?

_____

_____

What does the original Greek word for *patience* teach us about being patient?

_____

_____

Patience is not merely the ability to wait. What else is it?

_____

_____

When you are waiting for an answer, do you exhibit patience or frustration? If frustration, how can Hebrews 10:36 and James 1:4 help you find peace while you wait?

_____

_____

Think about this statement: "Some people dream of success, but others wake up and work hard at it." How have you found this to be true in your life when you've reached a goal after much waiting and work?

_____

_____

_____

Do You Have a Handicap?

Of the four temperaments mentioned, circle the one that seems to be dominant in you?

- The strong choleric
- The fun-loving sanguine
- The laid-back phlegmatic
- The deep, creative, but often dark melancholy

Based on your answer to the previous question, can you identify any natural weaknesses in your temperament that could prevent you from being more selfless? What are they, and how can you work with the Holy Spirit to not allow them to control you?

_____

_____

_____

What does it mean to have a "Spirit-controlled temperament"?

_____

_____

What are some of your strengths? What are some of your weaknesses? In what ways are you asking for help with your weaknesses?

_____

_____

Zacchaeus

How did Zacchaeus show determination when Jesus came to his town in Luke 19:1–5? What was the sign that this tax collector was ready to change?

_____

_____

Zacchaeus climbed a tree in order to see Jesus. What are you willing to do in order to see Him in your life?

_____

_____

_____

How can one visit from God change us forever? Have you ever experienced this or known someone who has? What happened?

_____

_____

_____

Be Relentless

How did blind Bartimaeus show relentlessness in Mark 10:46–52?

_____

_____

_____

Have you ever gotten excited about Jesus, and the religious people around you told you to calm down and be quiet? What did you do in that situation?

_____

_____

Is there something that is holding you back from stepping out in faith and allowing God to use you? What is it and how can you step out in faith in spite of it?

_____

_____

CHAPTER 15

Discover the Power of Caring for Others

Let each of you esteem and look upon and be concerned for not [merely]
his own interests, but also each for the interests of others.

Philippians 2:4

In Matthew 20:28, Jesus says He came to earth to serve instead of to be
served. What are some ways He served other people?

_____

_____

Why is it so difficult for people who are insecure and don't know who they
are in Christ to serve others?

_____

_____

_____

Fill in the blanks in this sentence from paragraph 4 of this section:
"I don't think any of us is truly _____ until we no
_____ feel the need to _____ anyone."

Among the people you associate with, are you a giver or taker? If you're a
taker, how can you become more giving?

_____

_____

_____

Why is it important for each person in a relationship to do things for the other person?

_____

_____

Why are "servant leaders" the best leaders of all?

_____

_____

Power in Serving

Does serving people come naturally to you? If not, what are some intentional ways you could help others?

_____

_____

What does 1 Peter 5:6 say about those who humble themselves?

_____

_____

What impressed you most about Darrell's story? What was the key to his transformation?

_____

_____

I Die Daily

In 1 Corinthians 15:31, Paul writes, "I die daily." What did he mean? Do you ever feel this way?

_____

_____

When we truly die to self, what kind of attitude do we have when we serve others?

_____

_____

Name something you have done recently, even when you didn't feel like doing it, to serve someone? How did you feel after you did it?

_____

_____

Fill in the blanks from Hebrews 13:16 NIV: "And do not _____ to do _____ and to _____ with others, for with such _____ God is _____."

Do you pray for God to show you what you can do for others? If not, try it today, and write down what God shows you.

_____

_____

Watch for Needs and Meet Them

Fill in the blanks in this sentence from paragraph 1 in this section: "Develop the _____ of paying _____ to what people say they _____ and _____."

Has anyone ever surprised you with a gift they heard you wanted? How did you feel? How can you do this for others?

_____

_____

Describe a time when you have given to someone and then realized that God has given back to you what you have given—many times over.

_____

_____

How have you seen these words from Anne Frank to be true: "No one has ever become poor by giving"?

_____

A Random Act of Kindness

Why is it important to live to give, not to get? How does this make us happy?

_____

_____

If you serve God in an unseen position and think you don't have a powerful role, how does the story of Stephen in Acts 6:1–8 inspire you?

_____

_____

What are some practical ways you could bear someone's burden, as Galatians 6:2 teaches us to do?

_____

_____

Here's a challenge for you: See how many unique ways you can serve or give. Be creative and have fun being a blessing to others.

Galatians 6:10 NIV says, "Therefore, as we have opportunity, let us do good to all people, especially those who belong to the family of believers." How can you do good to a fellow believer today?

_____

_____

A Simple Way Everyone Can Serve

What do you have at home that you are not using and that could benefit someone else?

_____

_____

As you read in *What About Me?*, "Our flesh loves to own things." If you enjoy owning things, how can you break this particular power of the flesh?

_____

_____

Why do you believe God loves to see people give and give generously?

_____

_____

Serving Is the Fruit of Loving God

In John 21:15–17, what did Jesus tell Peter to do to demonstrate his love for Him?

_____

_____

What so-called small things can you do for people this week?

_____

_____

What lessons can you learn from the fact that Jesus cooked breakfast for His disciples (John 21:12)?

_____

_____

Instead of thinking only about the *steps* of Jesus, what can you learn from thinking about the *stops* of Jesus?

_____

_____

_____

Do Everything for the Lord

Based on Colossians 3:23–24, do you need to make any changes in the way you approach your work or other things you do in life in order to do them for the Lord? If so, what are they?

_____

_____

_____

How difficult is it for you to serve others without wanting to impress some-one? Why?

_____

_____

From whom do we ultimately receive the rewards for the things we do?

_____

_____

When was the last time someone gave you a compliment or word of encour-agement? How did you feel? Who could you compliment or encourage this week?

_____

_____

Rate your listening skills on a scale of 1 to 10 (with 1 being the lowest and 10 being the highest).

1 2 3 4 5 6 7 8 9 10

Has anyone ever taken time to listen to you when you needed a sympathetic ear? How did that make you feel? Who can you take time to listen to this week?

_____

_____

How could you improve your listening skills?

_____

_____

CHAPTER 16

Fight Greed with Generosity

Guard yourselves and keep free from all covetousness (the immoderate desire for wealth, the greedy longing to have more); for a man's life does not consist in and is not derived from possessing overflowing abundance or that which is over and above his needs.

Luke 12:15

In your own words, what does Proverbs 1:19 mean?

_____

_____

How do we fight greed and selfishness?

_____

_____

With Luke 12:16–21 in mind, have you ever been tempted to "build a bigger barn" for yourself instead of helping others? What were the circumstances?

_____

_____

With your finances, do you "Give some, save some, and spend some within your borders"? Why or why not? Have you seen God expand your borders?

_____

_____

_____

Fill in the blanks in this sentence from the last paragraph of this section: "Excess in _____ area of life is the

_____ _____."

Generous People Get God's Attention

Tabitha, mentioned in Acts 9:36–41, was known for doing good deeds and helping the poor. Do you know someone who is known for the same reasons? Who is it? How might you help this person in their good deeds sometime soon?

_____

_____

According to Acts 10:4, why was Cornelius, a Gentile, the one chosen to send for Simon Peter? What blessing did he receive after Peter arrived?

_____

_____

Read Acts 4:32–35. Do you think this passage applies to us today? If yes, why don't more Christians practice it? If no, why not?

_____

_____

_____

Describe a time when have you been blessed by the generosity of fellow believers.

_____

_____

_____

How can you be generous to a fellow believer today?

_____

_____

_____

God Is Generous

What does *Jehovah-Jireh* mean? When has God shown Himself faithful to you in this way?

_____

_____

Why does God want you to grow spiritually before you grow materially?

_____

_____

In your own words, why is our giving important to God?

_____

_____

_____

Sowing and Reaping

Explain the kingdom principle of sowing and reaping based on Proverbs 18:24, Matthew 5:7, and Galatians 6:7–9. How can you sow into something you are hoping to reap?

_____

_____

_____

What could you give away in the next several weeks or months?

_____

_____

_____

According to James 1:27, what are the two categories of people God seems to have a special place in His heart for?

_____

_____

_____

Do you know any orphans or widows you could help? Check ideas from this list or come up with your own idea of how to help:

_____ Meet a financial need

_____ Include them in activities with your family

_____ Take them to lunch

_____ Buy them a gift card

Other: _____

Simone Weil said, "Attention is the rarest and purest form of generosity." Why do you think this is true? Who needs your attention this week?

_____

_____

Does your church have an outreach to the needy? If not, is this something you could help start? If you are not able to do so, what could you donate to a reputable ministry that serves the needy in your neighborhood or town?

_____

_____

Fill in the blanks in this sentence from the last paragraph of this section: "People who are never _____ with what they _____ will never be _____ even when they _____ what they _____."

Be Generous on Purpose

Do you plan your generosity? If not, here are some ways to start. Check the one(s) you think you can do this week:

_____ Think of people you can help.

_____ Listen to what people tell you they like or need.

_____ Spend time with someone who is lonely.

_____ Practice random acts of kindness.

_____ Donate money, clothing, or other items to shelters in your geographic area.

_____ Leave a generous tip.

_____ Send an encouraging note to someone.

_____ Start a giving fund.

Other: _____

What are the two tests we must pass concerning money?

1. _____

2. _____

How do we pass the two tests concerning money?

_____

_____

Generosity and Gratitude

Do you believe this statement: "We can never outgive God"? How have you found it to be true in your life?

_____

_____

Have you ever noticed the connection between gratitude and generosity? Explain it in your own words.

_____

_____

PART 5

"It's Really Not About Me"

CHAPTER 17

For the Love of God

Anyone who loves me will obey my teaching. My Father will love them, and we will come to them and make our home with them. Anyone who does not love me will not obey my teaching. These words you hear are not my own; they belong to the Father who sent me.

John 14:23–24 NIV

Is it possible to be selfish and self-centered and to walk in love at the same time? Explain your answer.

_____

_____

Why do we need to give special attention to our love walk?

_____

_____

Fill in the blanks from Matthew 22:37–40: "You shall _____ the Lord your God with all your _____ and with all your _____ and with all your _____ (intellect). This is the _____ (most important, principal) and _____ commandment. And a second is like it: You shall love your _____ as [you do] _____. These two _____ sum up and upon them depend all the Law and the Prophets."

What can you learn about love from 1 Timothy 1:5 and James 2:8 (ESV)?

_____

To overcome selfishness and self-centeredness, you could fight against them all the time. What's a better plan?

_____

_____

What is the positive way to deal with selfishness? What is the negative way?

_____

_____

_____

Based on the last sentence of this section, what will happen if we focus on doing the right thing?

_____

_____

_____

Receive God's Love and Give It Away

In 1 John 4:19 we read that God loved us before we loved Him. How has God shown you that He loves you?

_____

_____

What does Romans 5:5 teach us about God's love?

_____

_____

How can the awareness that God loves you help you learn to love yourself?

_____

_____

Do you regularly spend time in God's presence receiving His love for you? If not, a good way to start is simply to be quiet and spend a few minutes with God, thanking Him for His great love for you and asking Him to help you receive it.

According to 2 John 5–6 (NIV), what is love? What is God's command, which we "have heard from the beginning"?

_____

_____

We walk in love one step at a time. What specific steps can you take today to express love to the people around you?

_____

_____

How can you love someone today in the following ways?

- In your thoughts
- In your prayers
- With your words
- With your actions

Love and Sacrifice

Why does walking in love often require sacrifice?

_____

_____

_____

What have you had to sacrifice in order to show love to someone? Check all that apply.

_____ Time

_____ Energy

_____ Financial resources

_____ Material goods

_____ Your personal desires

Other:_____

What is the greatest reward you have received in exchange for some kind of sacrifice?

_____

_____

When you sacrifice to show love to someone, what should you focus on?

_____

_____

There are many ways to show people we love them. Which of these ways can help you show love today? Check all that apply.

_____ Be friendly

_____ Compliment them

_____ Help meet a need in their life

_____ Pray for them

_____ Be patient with their weaknesses

_____ Be quick to forgive them if they do something that hurts you

Other _____

In addition to the ways to show love that are listed above, what can you do in a specific way to show love to a specific person this week?

_____

_____

How can you show love to someone you may not particularly like?

_____

_____

Loving Yourself

Why does Jesus say we are to love our neighbor as we love ourselves (Matthew 22:37–40)?

_____

In your own words, what does it mean to love yourself but not be *in love* with yourself?

_____

_____

How can you love yourself while still being unselfish?

_____

_____

John, the Apostle of Love

Why is it encouraging to know that the apostle John, once known as one of the "Sons of Thunder," eventually became known as "the apostle of love"?

_____

_____

What can you learn about love from each of these Bible verses or passages?

- 1 John 3:10–11 NIV
- 1 John 3:14
- 1 John 3:16 NIV
- 1 John 3:17 NKJV
- 1 John 3:18

The Facets of Love

First Corinthians 13:4–8 (NIV) lists fifteen facets or qualities of love. What are they?

1. _____
2. _____
3. _____
4. _____

5. _____
6. _____
7. _____
8. _____
9. _____
10. _____
11. _____
12. _____
13. _____
14. _____
15. _____

Choose one or two facets of love and study them using God's Word or a dictionary. Which ones did you choose? What do they mean?

_____
_____

Love, Faith, and Forgiveness Work Together

What does it mean that faith works through love?

_____
_____

Why is forgiving others so important for us?

_____
_____

Why do many Christians feel justified in their anger and unforgiveness?

_____
_____

According to Luke 6:27–28, 35 and Romans 12:14, how should we treat our enemies (those who have hurt us, wronged us, or offended us)?

_____
_____

We Must Master Anger

Why can't people who are angry walk in love?

_____

_____

When you read that "Life is too short to spend it angry," what situation in your life comes to mind?

_____

_____

Why is it important not to allow your emotions to control you and to let the Holy Spirit guide you?

_____

_____

How can you apply Colossians 1:11 to your life right now?

_____

_____

_____

On a scale of 1–10, with 1 being "not at all" and 10 being "completely," how content are you when faced with circumstances you don't like?

1 2 3 4 5 6 7 8 9 10

Fill in the blank in this sentence from paragraph 5 of this section: "When people hurt you, they are hurting _____ more than they are hurting you."

What do these three Bible verses teach you about anger?

- James 1:20
- Proverbs 29:11
- Ecclesiastes 7:9

What does it mean that "Anger is a natural response to an injustice, and forgiveness is a supernatural response"?

_____

_____

Anger and Pride

In the first paragraph of this section, what are some descriptions of people who are proud? Do you see any of these qualities in yourself? If so, which ones?

_____

_____

How are anger and pride related?

_____

_____

What does this statement mean: "People who are proud and angry can pick their pain"?

_____

_____

CHAPTER 18

What About Me?

And Jesus called [to Him] the throng with His disciples and said to them, If anyone intends to come after Me, let him deny himself [forget, ignore, disown, and lose sight of himself and his own interests] and take up his cross, and [joining Me as a disciple and siding with My party] follow with Me [continually, cleaving steadfastly to Me].

Mark 8:34

After reading Mark 8:34, have you ever asked the question "What about me?" What answers can you glean from this Bible verse?

_____

_____

_____

As you are learning to obey Mark 8:34, how are you finding God to be faithful?

_____

_____

_____

Fill in the blanks in this sentence from the third paragraph of this section: "God does a much _____ job of taking care of _____ than we could ever do taking care of _____."

When you read 2 Corinthians 1:8–9 and 4:8–10, how does Paul's determination in the midst of sufferings encourage you as you go through various tests and trials?

_____

_____

Are you ready to surrender any "What about me?" attitude in yourself and trust God to take care of you? If so, pray this prayer: "Father, I surrender all to You, and I trust You to take care of me."

In your own words, explain what these words of George Müller's mean to you: "The beginning of anxiety is the end of faith, and the beginning of true faith is the end of anxiety."

_____

_____

_____

Read 1 Peter 5:7 (AMPC). What specific cares do you need to cast on God today?

_____

_____

_____

What does it mean to enter God's rest?

_____

_____

_____

The English word *rest* comes from the Greek word *anapauo*. What does this word mean?

_____

_____

_____

On a scale of 1 to 10, with 1 being "not much" and 10 being "almost completely," how much would you say you trust God?

1 2 3 4 5 6 7 8 9 10

Trust is based on what we know about the character of the person we trust. What do you know about God's character that gives you confidence in being able to trust Him?

_____

_____

True or false: It is possible to trust God and to be anxious or worried at the same time. Explain your answer.

_____

_____

How have you gradually developed trust in God?

_____

_____

_____

Faith Is Required

Why does living a lifestyle of casting our cares on God and trusting Him require faith?

_____

_____

_____

What do we learn about God's mercies in Lamentations 3:22–23?

_____

_____

_____

Since "Faith is not the absence of fear; it is often moving forward while you still feel afraid," describe a time when you decided to follow God and "do it afraid."

_____

_____

_____

Fill in the blanks in this sentence from the fourth paragraph of this section: "Faith requires _____ with no _____ that God is _____ anything at all."

These scriptures encourage us that God will take care of us. What can you learn from each one?

- Psalm 37:4 ESV
- Psalm 23:1 NKJV
- Matthew 6:33 NLT
- Philippians 4:19 NKJV
- Romans 8:32 NIV

Romans 10:17 (NKJV) teaches us that faith comes by hearing the Word of God. What can you do in a practical way to hear more of God's Word each day?

_____

_____

What If I Don't Get What I Want?

What is the root of our reluctance to trust God completely?

_____

_____

_____

If you are not getting what you're hoping for, do you trust that God loves you and has your best interests at heart? Do you also trust that He has something better in mind for you? Describe the situation.

_____

_____

_____

Why is it sometimes better for us not to get what we want and learn to be content anyway?

_____

_____

If you have children, how do you feel when they don't trust you when you tell them they can't have something? How do you think God feels when you don't trust Him when you don't get what you want?

_____

_____

Fill in the blanks in this sentence from the third-to-last paragraph of this section: "Trusting God does not _____ we will get what we _____, but it does guarantee that we will get what is _____ for us at the _____ _____."

What would help you trust that God's will is better than yours?

_____

_____

How often do you pray "Help me, Lord" in a day? Why is this simple prayer one of the most powerful ones we can pray?

_____

_____

CHAPTER 19

Resurrection Power

Behold! I have given you authority and power to trample upon serpents and scorpions, and [physical and mental strength and ability] over all the power that the enemy [possesses]; and nothing shall in any way harm you.

Luke 10:19

We need God's power to live a life of sacrifice and love. What happens when you try in your own strength to live this way?

_____

_____

Why did Paul want to experience the power of Christ's resurrection in Philippians 3:10?

_____

_____

Fill in the blanks in this sentence from paragraph 5 of this section: "We can live _____ in this world and be _____ and _____, no matter what is going on around us."

List some ways to achieve continual fellowship with Jesus and retain spiritual power.

_____

_____

Stopped-Up Wells

Think of having "rivers of living water" flowing from you for others to drink from. Draw a stick figure of yourself and from it lines representing your flow reaching others. At the end of each line, write the name of the person receiving it. How powerful and abundant is your flow? Are there any blockages?

List the 10 ways the devil tries to "stop up our wells."

_____

_____

What are some ways spiritually weak people allow their power to be diluted? Explain.

_____

_____

How could selfishness stop up your well?

_____

_____

Explain this statement: "Selfishness renders us weak, but love is the most powerful force in the world."

_____

_____

Helping Others Helps You Deal with Your Problems

What impressed you about Donna's story? How did serving at the adult day care help her? How has serving others when you were suffering helped you?

_____

_____

_____

God used Donna's service to transform her heart. How could that have been a factor in her husband's transformation?

_____

_____

Disobedience

Why can disobedience be like stones stopping up your well? Imagine a well filled with stones. Now imagine trying to draw out water. Ask God to reveal any stones that are stopping up your well, then repent of anything He shows you.

_____

_____

In Isaiah 48:18, why didn't the Israelites achieve peace and prosperity?

_____

_____

_____

According to Exodus 23:22, under what circumstances will God defeat your enemies?

_____

_____

_____

What's the main thing you must do to keep God's power flowing in your life?

_____

_____

_____

Go into a dark room and try to find something without turning on the light. Now think of living the Christian life without "turning on" God's power. What will happen?

_____

_____

_____

If you haven't already asked God to fill you with the Holy Spirit, do so now. Then start believing His power is in you and that you can do things you would not ordinarily be able to do. Study this list often:

- You can go through difficult situations and still walk in the fruit of the Holy Spirit, trust God, and love people.
- You can resist any kind of temptation because God will never allow you to be tempted beyond what you can bear (1 Corinthians 10:13).
- You can live a surrendered life and be content and joyful.
- You can live totally free from unforgiveness and offense because when people hurt you, you are more concerned about what they are doing to themselves than what they are doing to you (Luke 23:34).
- You can live unselfishly, sacrificially, and not think, *What about me?*
- You can enter God's rest and enjoy life even if your circumstances are difficult.

Power, Love, and a Sound Mind

List three things 2 Timothy 1:7 says you have as a follower of Jesus. List the one thing the verse says you don't have.

_____

_____

What Do You Believe about Yourself?

Why is false humility not good for a Christian? Pray and ask God to help you understand who you are in Christ and then ask Him to help you live like you know who you are.

_____

_____

_____

Describe a situation when you believe God heard you and answered your prayers (Mark 11:24).

_____

_____

Do you believe God loves you unconditionally and has a good plan for your life (Jeremiah 29:11; 1 John 4:16)? Give an example of how God has shown His love to you.

_____

_____

Do you believe you are the head and not the tail, above and not beneath (Deuteronomy 28:13; Ephesians 1:18–23)? Explain your answer.

_____

_____

Do you believe God has forgiven and forgotten your sins (Isaiah 43:25; Ephesians 1:7)? Explain your answer.

_____

_____

Do you have the confidence to step out and try new things without fearing failure (Isaiah 41:10)? Describe one of those new things you want to step into.

_____

_____

Why does the devil want to prevent you from believing these truths? How can you defeat his lies?

_____

_____

_____

True or false: If I feel weak and defeated, I don't have God's power. Explain your answer.

_____

_____

_____

Power Belongs to You

Fill in the blanks in this sentence from the last paragraph of this section: "God's _____ belongs to you, and you need to see yourself as _____, _____, _____, and _____."

Why can you never go beyond what you believe about yourself?

_____

_____

Say aloud, several times each day, "God's power is in me. I am strong in the Lord, and I can do whatever I need to do in life through Christ."

CHAPTER 20

This Hurts!

The saying is sure and worthy of confidence: If we have died with Him, we shall also live with Him.

2 Timothy 2:11

Would you agree with the statement: "It hurts to grow up"? How have you experienced this personally or seen it in someone close to you?

_____

_____

Why is it painful to grow up spiritually?

_____

_____

How did the "honeymoon phase" of your relationship with God differ from the way things are now in your relationship with Him? Why does the honeymoon phase eventually end, and what does it mean when we realize things aren't so easy anymore?

_____

Based on Acts 20:1, what four things did Paul do to inspire spiritual growth in the disciples after he sent for them?

1. _____

2. _____

3. _____

4. _____

Death Brings Life

In your own words, based on what you've learned so far, what does this statement mean: "Dying to self means dying to our way and accepting God's way"?

_____

_____

What are some examples of dying to self in your daily life right now?

_____

_____

_____

According to 2 Timothy 2:11, we are dead to sin. So why do we still have the temptation to sin (Matthew 26:41)?

_____

_____

_____

If selfishness is a sin, what changes do you need to make in your life?

_____

_____

_____

Work Out Your Salvation

If you never have to work for your salvation because it is a gift of God's grace, why does Philippians 2:12 teach that you have to "work out" your salvation?

_____

_____

_____

Fill in the blanks in this sentence from the third paragraph of this section: "We must work _____ what God has worked _____ us by His grace."

What are some ways you can work out your salvation in front of those who are watching your life?

_____

_____

Philippians 2:12–13 states that we should work with the Holy Spirit enthusiastically to work out and complete our salvation with "reverence and awe and trembling." What does this mean?

_____

_____

The Salvation of the Soul

What does it mean to submit and surrender our will to God?

_____

_____

Which of these areas have you surrendered and submitted to the Holy Spirit? Check all that apply, and ask God to help you surrender the others.

_____ The use of your time, even your leisure time

_____ The entertainment you approve of and participate in

_____ The ways you spend your money

_____ Your thoughts

_____ Your mouth and the words you speak

_____ Your attitudes

_____ What you read and watch

_____ How you treat other people

If you aren't sure what God's will is in a particular area, this checklist can help you remember to analyze your choices. Commit to asking yourself these questions often:

- Am I in too big of a hurry to hear God if He speaks?
- Am I doing what God desires and behaving in ways that please Him?
- Am I doing anything that bothers my conscience?
- Am I at peace with the choices I am making today?

If you fail in your efforts to put to death the works of the flesh, how many times should you try again? Explain your answer.

_____

_____

God's Toolbox

What are some of the tools God has used to help you die to self and submit to His authority? Check all that apply.

_____ Situations out of your control

_____ People telling you to do things you don't want to do

_____ People with difficult or irritating personalities

_____ Submitting to your spouse

_____ Submitting to civil authorities

_____ Not receiving the recognition or lifestyle you think you deserve

Other: _____

Circumstances beyond Our Control

According to Isaiah 41:10, how does God use circumstances beyond your control to benefit you?

_____

_____

What does 1 Peter 4:12 say could be the reason you are suffereing with various problems?

_____

_____

Fill in the blanks in this sentence from the second-to-last paragraph of this section: "God wants us to be _____ to Him, but _____ to the devil."

What fruit of the Spirit can come out of trials if we handle them well (James 1:2–3)? How will developing this fruit help you?

_____

_____

Divine Disappointments

Why does God allow disappointments in your life? What disappointment(s) has He turned to good in your life?

_____

_____

How can you tell the difference between a trial arranged by God and an attack from the devil? How would you handle a trial arranged by God differently than you would handle an attack from the enemy?

_____

_____

CHAPTER 21

The Living Dead

Whereas she who lives in pleasure and self-gratification [giving herself up to luxury and self-indulgence] is dead even while she [still] lives.

1 Timothy 5:6

According to 1 Timothy 5:6, what happens to people who live to make themselves happy? What does this mean?

_____

_____

What happened to Adam and Eve when they disobeyed God?

_____

_____

According to 1 John 3:14, what happens to people spiritually (not physically) when they do not love?

_____

_____

What does it mean, spiritually, to pass from death to life?

_____

_____

Have you ever encountered people who seem to be "the walking dead"? What are they like?

_____

_____

Romans 12:21 teaches that we overcome evil with what?

_____

_____

Dead Man Walking

How does being selfish lead to loneliness?

_____

_____

Why is selfishness like living in solitary confinement?

_____

_____

As believers in Christ, what two qualities of His are now in us?

1. _____

2. _____

In your own words, what does Mark 8:34 mean?

_____

_____

What happens when we do things God's way?

_____

_____

_____

Three Ways to Express Love to People

What are three ways we can express love to other people?

_____

_____

_____

Fill in the blanks from Luke 6:36: "So be merciful (_____,

_____, _____, and _____) even

as your Father is [all these]."

What makes it easier to show mercy to other people?

_____

_____

Based on the first paragraph under the subheading "Be Merciful," describe in your own words what mercy is.

_____

_____

God's mercies are new every morning (Lamentations 3:22–23 ESV). How has God been merciful to you?

_____

_____

Are you receiving God's new mercies every morning, or are you still punishing yourself for mistakes you have made? Explain your answer. If so, remember that His mercies are available to you today and every day.

_____

_____

How does Hebrews 2:17 describe Jesus?

_____

_____

When you think about who Jesus is, according to Hebrews 2:17, how do you feel?

_____

_____

Think about a specific relationship in your life: How would that relationship be easier if both people were to show mercy to each other?

_____

_____

Do you believe that being angry is harder on us than on the person we are angry with? Why or why not?

_____

_____

Why do you feel this statement is true: "We could eliminate so much fear in the world if people could count on one another for mercy instead of punishment"? How might this apply in your personal life?

_____

_____

Who in your life needs to experience mercy? How can you show mercy to them?

_____

_____

How can you show mercy to someone while also allowing them to experience appropriate consequences of their behavior?

_____

_____

When God must chastise us, why does He do it, according to Hebrews 12:6 and Revelation 3:19?

_____

_____

What does this sentence mean to you, and how can you apply it in your life: "The fact that He is merciful does not remove our responsibility to do the best we can, but it does give us an opportunity to repent and make a change for the better"?

_____

_____

How does God's mercy toward you bring you joy? How could your mercy toward someone else bring them joy?

_____

_____

As you read Psalm 145:8–9 and Psalm 136:23–24, what stands out to you about God and the way He loves us?

_____

_____

What does it mean to "put on tender mercies" (Colossians 3:12 NKJV)?

_____

_____

According to Colossians 3:13 (ESV), why must we forgive others?

_____

_____

When we refuse to forgive, we may think we are punishing those who hurt us, but why are we actually imprisoning ourselves in hatred and bitterness?

_____

_____

True or false: Forgiveness is a feeling, not a decision.
What happens when you forgive an offender?

_____

_____

Do you need to forgive someone today? If so, simply make the decision to forgive, and pray this simple prayer or a similar one: "God, it isn't easy, but today I choose to forgive _____ for _____. Set me free from unforgiveness and help me walk in forgiveness continually. In Jesus' name. Amen."

Why is it important not to judge people?

_____

_____

According to 1 Corinthians 13:7, what does love always believe about other people?

_____

_____

Developing Loving Attitudes

Does being merciful, forgiving, and nonjudgmental come naturally to you, or do you find yourself having to develop loving attitudes? Explain your answer.

_____

_____

According to Matthew 5:7, what happens to those who are merciful?

_____

_____

True or false: No one really has the right to judge another person. What is the difference between judging a person and judging sin?

_____

_____

In your own words, what does Ephesians 2:4–5 mean?

_____

_____

Complete this sentence from the last paragraph of chapter 21: "God's ways bring _____ and _____." What happens if we do not operate in God's ways?

_____

_____

CHAPTER 22

Complete Surrender

I appeal to you therefore, brethren, and beg of you in view of [all] the mercies of God, to make a decisive dedication of your bodies [presenting all your members and faculties] as a living sacrifice, holy (devoted, consecrated) and well pleasing to God, which is your reasonable (rational, intelligent) service and spiritual worship.

Romans 12:1

Several words or phrases in Romans 12:1 stand out. What does each one mean to you?

- decisive
- dedication
- living sacrifice
- holy and devoted
- consecrated
- well pleasing to God
- service
- worship

Complete surrender is a big commitment. When you think of the word *commitment*, what comes to mind? When have you committed to something or someone? Are you making good on that commitment?

If you have not yet surrendered every area of your life to God, what's holding you back?

_____

_____

If you are serious about making a complete surrender, write it down and note the date. For example, "On (date), I surrender my body and every area of my life to You, God." Think about your commitment regularly and ask God to help you fulfill it.

_____

_____

Change

How can you relate to this observation: "We often want our circumstances to change, but _we_ don't want to change"?

_____

_____

Why won't our circumstances change until we do? How has this been true for you?

_____

_____

_____

When you are born again, why doesn't your soul automatically transform with your spirit? What part do you need to play in soul transformation?

_____

_____

_____

Review this definition in the second paragraph of this section by filling in the blanks: "Dying to self is no longer living according to what we

_____, _____, and _____."

What does Romans 6:11 mean when it says you are "dead to sin," when sin still exists?

_____

_____

Fill in the blanks in the first sentence of paragraph 3 of this section: "God's desire is to not only _____ us but also to _____ us." What does this mean to you?

_____

_____

How does Colossians 1:13–14 give you hope?

_____

_____

When you realize how God is trying to transform you through dying to self, how does that make you think differently about this difficult process?

_____

_____

Metamorphosis

Fill in the blanks in this sentence from paragraph 1 of this section: "When we are _____, we are no longer what we once _____, but we are not yet what we _____ _____."

What comes to mind when you think of metamorphosis?

_____

_____

_____

What similarities do you see between a caterpillar's transformation and your being changed into the image of Christ?

_____

_____

What are some ways you feel God has kept you in a cocoon too long when you longed to be set free? How was the wait worth it?

_____

_____

_____

Changed into the Image of Christ

Which of these changes have you seen in your own life? Put a checkmark by the ones you have seen and an x by the ones you're still working on.

_____ Doing what is godly

_____ Making godly choices

_____ Speaking in godly ways

_____ Having godly attitudes

_____ Treating people well

_____ Using money and other resources wisely

According to Galatians 2:20 (NKJV), what does it mean to "die to live"?

_____

_____

_____

Describe a time when you have practiced what this statement says: "I don't have to feel like doing the right thing to do it."

_____

_____

_____

According to the last paragraph of this section, what are the two main truths from this book that will help you when you are faced with making difficult decisions?

_____

_____

The Teacup Story

What lessons did you learn from the "Teacup Story"?

_____

_____

Have you ever felt like the teacup did in the oven, wanting to escape the heat? Explain your answer.

_____

_____

Describe a time when you have felt like giving up on the whole transformation process. What encouraged you to keep going?

_____

_____

How has God made you beautiful?

_____

_____

CONCLUSION

Learning to live unselfishly is a lifetime journey. I have been on this journey for many years, and I am still on it. I have seen a lot of improvement as God has helped me move toward unselfish living, but I am not perfect, and I don't think any of us will be as long as we live on earth.

I hope you have learned a lot about yourself and the way you treat others as you've worked your way through this study guide based on my book, *What About Me?* I encourage you to pray regularly about the issue of selfishness. Ask God to help you live an unselfish life, and follow the Holy Spirit as He helps you break free from living based on what you want, what you think, and what you feel.

Because unselfish living is a marathon, not a sprint, I hope you'll consider reading *What About Me?* more than once and working through this study guide again in the future. It would be very interesting to see how your responses might be different a year from now compared to what they are today.

I am praying God will help you and bless you as you learn to live more unselfishly, because I know that the more we focus on others instead of ourselves, the more joyful life is.

Do you have a real relationship with Jesus?

God loves you! He created you to be a special, unique, one-of-a-kind individual, and He has a specific purpose and plan for your life. And through a personal relationship with your Creator—God—you can discover a way of life that will truly satisfy your soul.

No matter who you are, what you've done, or where you are in your life right now, God's love and grace are greater than your sin—your mistakes. Jesus willingly gave His life so you can receive forgiveness from God and have new life in Him. He's just waiting for you to invite Him to be your Savior and Lord.

If you are ready to commit your life to Jesus and follow Him, all you have to do is ask Him to forgive your sins and give you a fresh start in the life you are meant to live. Begin by praying this prayer...

> *Lord Jesus, thank You for giving Your life for me and forgiving me of my sins so I can have a personal relationship with You. I am sincerely sorry for the mistakes I've made, and I know I need You to help me live right.*

> *Your Word says in Romans 10:9, "If you declare with your mouth, 'Jesus is Lord,' and believe in your heart that God raised him from the dead, you will be saved" (NIV). I believe You are the Son of God and confess You as my Savior and Lord. Take me just as I am, and work in my heart, making me the person You want me to be. I want to live for You, Jesus, and I am so grateful that You are giving me a fresh start in my new life with You today.*

> *I love You, Jesus!*

It's so amazing to know that God loves us so much! He wants to have a deep, intimate relationship with us that grows every day as we spend time with Him in prayer and Bible study. And we want to encourage you in your new life in Christ.

Please visit joycemeyer.org/salvation to request Joyce's book *A New Way of Living*, which is our gift to you. We also have other free resources online to help you make progress in pursuing everything God has for you.

Congratulations on your fresh start in your life in Christ! We hope to hear from you soon.

NOTES

ABOUT THE AUTHOR

Joyce Meyer is one of the world's leading practical Bible teachers and a *New York Times* bestselling author. Joyce's books have helped millions of people find hope and restoration through Jesus Christ. Joyce's program, *Enjoying Everyday Life,* is broadcast on television, radio, and online to millions worldwide in 110 languages.

Through Joyce Meyer Ministries, Joyce teaches internationally on a number of topics with a particular focus on how the Word of God applies to our everyday lives. Her candid communication style allows her to share openly and practically about her experiences so others can apply what she has learned to their lives.

Joyce has authored more than 140 books, which have been translated into more than 160 languages, and over 41 million of her books have been distributed worldwide. Bestsellers include *Power Thoughts*; *The Confident Woman*; *Look Great, Feel Great*; *Starting Your Day Right*; *Ending Your Day Right*; *Approval Addiction*; *How to Hear from God*; *Beauty for Ashes*; and *Battlefield of the Mind.*

Joyce's passion to help people who are hurting is foundational to the vision of Hand of Hope, the missions arm of Joyce Meyer Ministries. Each year Hand of Hope provides millions of meals for the hungry and malnourished, installs freshwater wells in poor and remote areas, provides critical relief after natural disasters, and offers free medical and dental care to thousands through their hospitals and clinics worldwide. Through Project GRL, women and children are rescued from human trafficking and provided safe places to receive an education, nutritious meals, and the love of God.

JOYCE MEYER MINISTRIES
U.S. & FOREIGN OFFICE ADDRESSES

Joyce Meyer Ministries
P.O. Box 655
Fenton, MO 63026
USA
(866) 480-1528

Joyce Meyer Ministries—Canada
P.O. Box 7700
Vancouver, BC V6B 4E2
Canada
(800) 868-1002

Joyce Meyer Ministries—Australia
Locked Bag 77
Mansfield Delivery Centre
Queensland 4122
Australia
+61 7 3349 1200

Joyce Meyer Ministries—England
P.O. Box 8267
Reading RG6 9TX
United Kingdom
+44 1753 831102

Joyce Meyer Ministries—South Africa
Unit EB06, East Block, Tannery Park
23 Belmont Road
Rondebosch, Cape Town, South Africa, 7700
+27 21 701 1056

Joyce Meyer Ministries—Francophonie
29 avenue Maurice Chevalier
77330 Ozoir la Ferriere
France

Joyce Meyer Ministries—Germany
Postfach 761001
22060 Hamburg
Germany
+49 (0)40 / 88 88 4 11 11

Joyce Meyer Ministries—Netherlands
Postbus 55
7000 HB Doetinchem
The Netherlands
+31 (0)26 20 22 100

Joyce Meyer Ministries—Russia
P.O. Box 789
Moscow 101000
Russia
+7 (495) 727-14-68

OTHER BOOKS BY JOYCE MEYER

100 Inspirational Quotes
100 Ways to Simplify Your Life
21 Ways to Finding Peace and Happiness
The Answer to Anxiety
Any Minute
Approval Addiction
The Approval Fix
Authentically, Uniquely You*
The Battle Belongs to the Lord
Battlefield of the Mind*
Battlefield of the Mind Bible
Battlefield of the Mind for Kids
Battlefield of the Mind for Teens
Battlefield of the Mind Devotional
Battlefield of the Mind New Testament
Be Anxious for Nothing*
Being the Person God Made You to Be
Beauty for Ashes
Change Your Words, Change Your Life
Colossians: A Biblical Study
The Confident Mom
The Confident Woman
The Confident Woman Devotional
Do It Afraid*
Do Yourself a Favor . . . Forgive
Eat the Cookie . . . Buy the Shoes
Eight Ways to Keep the Devil under Your Feet
Ending Your Day Right
Enjoying Where You Are on the Way to Where You Are Going
Ephesians: A Biblical Study
The Everyday Life Bible
The Everyday Life Psalms and Proverbs
Filled with the Spirit
Finding God's Will for Your Life
Galatians: A Biblical Study
Good Health, Good Life
Habits of a Godly Woman
Healing the Soul of a Woman*
Healing the Soul of a Woman Devotional
Hearing from God Each Morning
How to Age without Getting Old

*How to Hear from God**
How to Succeed at Being Yourself
How to Talk with God
I Dare You
*If Not for the Grace of God**
In Pursuit of Peace
In Search of Wisdom
James: A Biblical Study
The Joy of Believing Prayer
Knowing God Intimately
A Leader in the Making
Life in the Word
Living beyond Your Feelings
Living Courageously
Look Great, Feel Great
Love Out Loud
The Love Revolution
Loving People Who Are Hard to Love
Making Good Habits, Breaking Bad Habits
Managing Your Emotions
Making Marriage Work (previously published as *Help Me—I'm Married!*)
*Me and My Big Mouth!**
*The Mind Connection**
Never Give Up!
Never Lose Heart
New Day, New You
Overcoming Every Problem
Overload
The Pathway to Success
The Penny
Perfect Love (previously published as *God Is Not Mad at You*)*
Philippians: A Biblical Study
The Power of Being Positive
The Power of Being Thankful
The Power of Determination
The Power of Forgiveness
The Power of Simple Prayer
Power Thoughts
Power Thoughts Devotional
Powerful Thinking
Quiet Times with God Devotional
Reduce Me to Love
The Secret Power of Speaking God's Word

The Secrets of Spiritual Power
The Secret to True Happiness
Seven Things That Steal Your Joy
Start Your New Life Today
Starting Your Day Right
Straight Talk
Teenagers Are People Too!
Trusting God Day by Day
The Word, the Name, the Blood
Woman to Woman
You Can Begin Again
Your Battles Belong to the Lord*

JOYCE MEYER SPANISH TITLES

Amar a la gente que es muy difícil de amar (Loving People Who Are Hard to Love)
Auténtica y única (Authentically, Uniquely You)
Belleza en lugar de cenizas (Beauty for Ashes)
Bendicion en el desorden (Blessed in the Mess)
Buena salud, buena vida (Good Health, Good Life)
Cambia tus palabras, cambia tu vida (Change Your Words, Change Your Life)
El campo de batalla de la mente (Battlefield of the Mind)
Cómo envejecer sin avejentarse (How to Age without Getting Old)
Como formar buenos habitos y romper malos habitos (Making Good Habits, Breaking Bad Habits)
La conexión de la mente (The Mind Connection)
Dios no está enojado contigo (God Is Not Mad at You)
La dosis de aprobación (The Approval Fix)
Efesios: Comentario biblico (Ephesians: Biblical Commentary)
Empezando tu día bien (Starting Your Day Right)
Hágalo con miedo (Do It Afraid)
Hazte un favor a ti mismo… perdona (Do Yourself a Favor… Forgive)
Madre segura de sí misma (The Confident Mom)
Momentos de quietud con Dios (Quiet Times with God Devotional)
Mujer segura de sí misma (The Confident Woman)
No se afane por nada (Be Anxious for Nothing)
Pensamientos de poder (Power Thoughts)
Sanidad para el alma de una mujer (Healing the Soul of a Woman)
Sanidad para el alma de una mujer, devocionario (Healing the Soul of a Woman Devotional)
Santiago: Comentario bíblico (James: Biblical Commentary)
Sobrecarga (Overload)*

Sus batallas son del Señor (Your Battles Belong to the Lord)
Termina bien tu día (Ending Your Day Right)
Tienes que atreverte (I Dare You)
Usted puede comenzar de nuevo (You Can Begin Again)
Viva amando su vida (Living a Life You Love)
Viva valientemente (Living Courageously)
Vive por encima de tus sentimientos (Living beyond Your Feelings)
* Study Guide available for this title

BOOKS BY DAVE MEYER

Life Lines